STARVED
FOR
BOOKS

The story of how American librarians, children, the rich, the poor, and others collected millions of books for soldiers fighting in World War II.

Carole Marsh Longmeyer

Let There Be Learning Books
Beaufort, South Carolina, USA

Library of Congress Cataloging-in-Publication Data is available.
ISBN 978-0-635-14170-5

Book design and illustrations by Lee Barrow

Printed in the United States of America

Public domain and other credits appear at end of book.

Dedicated to librarians then and now and in the future.

CONTENTS

STARVED
FOR
BOOKS

During World War II,

if you could have peeked at young soldiers standing in the chow line...sitting idly waiting for battle orders...impatiently standing on one foot, then the other, for a haircut...or even up to their neck in a muddy foxhole, you might have seen each one with something you would not expect.

No, not a helmet or rifle, but...a book. Worn, tattered, much read, shared, and beloved books. Perhaps they were tucked in a back pocket, stuck inside a field jacket, or held right in front of their face. These books were important. And how all these books got to all those soldiers is a fascinating story!

Before we begin this story,

think a minute about books. What does a book mean to you? It might mean schoolwork or homework, studying for a test, even a boring chore to read, if you are not an avid reader.

To some of you, a book may mean a chance to escape on an adventure, an afternoon in the hammock reading a favorite story, or a gift for a best friend's birthday.

To others, books may be essential. Without a book in hand, you may feel like a part of you is missing. Books may be transformative, even lifesaving. They may be our temporary sanity, or at the least, a distraction, even joy.

Whether we are book crazy or not, we know that books are important. Yes, some are better written than others, but all count as part of our literature. Can we even imagine life without libraries filled with books?

A man named Adolph Hitler could. He once had more than 100 million books burned in enormous bonfires. Why? Because he thought that only he knew which books were worthy to exist. In other words, he thought he knew best—for everyone.

That sounds crazy, doesn't it? But he knew that he was not just burning books, but also destroying ideas that he did not agree with. Or, at least he thought he was. However, although you can burn paper easily, it is not that easy to destroy the ideas, thoughts, or hard-written words of writers.

All this happened in Germany during World War II. The book burnings were a wake-up call to Americans, who were not involved in the war at that time. One of the ideas that Adolph Hitler wanted to burn and destroy was democracy. Americans knew Hitler was very mistaken—he might burn books, but he could not destroy democratic ideas. American citizens began to pay more attention to what was going on in Europe. And then one day, the nation of Japan bombed the U.S. air base at Pearl Harbor in Hawaiʻi and America went to war!

We went to war to protect lives, to protest killing and taking other peoples' lands, and to save ideas like democracy and freedom from destruction. And, to save the books.

World War II: *(also called the Second World War; often abbreviated WWII)* a global war between the Allies and the Axis countries that lasted from 1939-1945.

I am so bored...always waiting around...it gets on my nerves. If I had a good book to read, it sure would help pass the time.

I am so tired. Sometimes, I just wish I could sit down and read a good book. Ever felt that way?

I am so scared! War is horrible. I have seen my buddies killed in battle. I need to read something good, something that reminds me of home and peace and hope for a good future. I need a book.

I am so lonesome. I miss my family. I wish I had a book to read to take my mind off war.

I am just starved for books!

Librarian Super Heroes to the Rescue!

Now who do you imagine might be the most upset at the burning of books? Librarians, of course! Librarians across America were angry at the very thought that someone like Adolph Hitler would believe that he could permanently erase good ideas, thoughts, stories, poems, novels, textbooks and more, just by burning them.

Librarians decided that their best weapon was...THE BOOK! If Germany was going to burn books, and also spread a lot of propaganda against the ideas in those books, then librarians would fight back!

First, they encouraged Americans to read, read, read! To read and learn about the war. To read and learn about all kinds of things. To read for fun and joy. And, especially, to read and understand how wrong intolerance, oppression, and hate are.

Librarians dedicated themselves to share and preserve good ideas, the fairness of democracy, and the value of books and freedom of speech. But they also had another idea!

---

propaganda: biased and often misleading information used to influence readers to believe in a particular opinion.

Poster against book burning, 1942

The Great Book Drive—Part I

Many librarians (then and now) belonged to The American Library Association, the ALA. They realized that if they worked together they would have more power to protect and preserve books.

However, they wanted to do more than that. During World War II, they heard that U.S. soldiers were "starved for books." Sadly, there were almost no books in the hands of soldiers—not on their bases and not overseas with them on the war fronts. The librarians set out to remedy that.

They encouraged the collection of hundreds and thousands of books to send to soldiers. Americans thought this was a great idea. Soon, donation boxes and bins were set up in libraries, schools, department stores, movie theaters, and everywhere else possible.

While Germany burned books, America put on the largest book drive ever undertaken in the history of the world!

Rosie the Riveter poster, 1942

A girl donating books at Penn Station in New York City, 1942

A Look Back

Let's take a look back at what else was happening during this time in history.

You may be surprised to learn that while all these things were going on—war, book burnings, book collecting—America was not yet at war with Germany.

As this war—the country of Germany against other nations—spread slowly in 1939 and 1940, most Americans did not see any reason or need to get involved in a war "over there" across the Atlantic Ocean.

Nonetheless, enough people felt that America should at least be prepared for war. To help that, a national draft was started. This meant that men between the ages of 21-35 had to register for military service—just in case they were needed.

Imagine if you had been the age you are now back then. Your father, brother, uncle, friends, and neighbors might have had to register for this compulsory draft.

---

compulsory: something you are required to do, often by law

Why was the conscription of men for military service so essential? Because at that time, the U.S. Armed Forces had less than 200,000 active duty soldiers. That was not nearly enough to fight a war or defend our nation.

---

conscription: compulsory enlistment in the military

In September 1940, the U.S. Congress passed the Selective Training and Service Act. More than 16 million men registered for the draft. While the draft was not popular, everyone understood that America had no choice but to prepare for war. And it's a good thing that we did.

Soon, new soldiers found themselves in bare-bones training camps, with lots of rules, waiting, wondering, and worrying what was going to happen next. While the last thing on the military's mind was books, books were at the top of the list of what the new soldiers wanted. To boys far from home, lonesome for family and friends, and often bored to tears, nothing seemed more of a treasure than a book to escape with, even for a short time.

Wars Before and Books Before

Does it seem strange to you that most soldiers would crave books over a movie, sports equipment, or even listening to a radio? Imagine that you are packed with other soldiers in your barracks...marching shoulder to shoulder on the field...training with other troops all day...eating your meals, going to the bathroom, showering, and almost everything else you had once done at home in peace and privacy—with other hot, sweaty, and tired soldiers.

Soldiers were desperate for peace and quiet, a way to at least pretend that they were alone for a little while and thinking about something besides war. A book would be a good solution, don't you think?

Even in the U.S. Civil War, soldiers were said to "hunger and thirst" for books. During World War I, soldiers also craved books. The Red Cross, YMCA (Young Men's Christian Association) and YWCA (Young Women's Christian Association), Salvation Army, and other organizations worked to provide books. The soldiers said that books made "life worth living" as they attempted to survive battle, wounds, loneliness, and discouragement.

WAR CHART

Revolutionary War.....1775–1783
Civil War.....1861–1865
Spanish–American War.....1898
World War I.....1914–1918
WORLD WAR II.....1939–1945
Korean War.....1950–1953
Vietnam War.....1955–1975
Gulf War.....1990–1991
Afghanistan War.....2001–2021
Iraq War.....2003–2011

In 1921, the Army Library Service had 228 libraries at Army posts around the country. However, as the number of soldiers diminished over the years, the libraries were neglected. Many of the few books on the shelves were outdated, worn out, and boring.

Almost 20 years later, a soldier with a professional library college degree was put in charge of the Library Section of the United States Army. Raymond Trautman had also managed bookstores. This librarian did not like that larger posts got lots of books, while training camps had almost no books. Soon, he had book drives going on by many librarians. Thousands of books were collected and sent to soldiers. But even "thousands" of books were just a drop in the bucket of what was needed.

Very soon, things changed!

The Great Book Drive—Part II

As word continued to get out of how important books were to the soldiers' morale, the members of the American Library Association just could not accept empty library shelves for soldiers.

They soon went to work on a goal to collect MILLIONS of books, and as fast as possible. With the help of the USO (United Service Organizations) and the American Red Cross, the ALA's National Defense Book Campaign was begun.

Their office was in the Empire State Building in New York City. Althea Warren, a librarian, was put in charge of the NDBC book drive. An enthusiastic book lover, she knew that books were as essential to soldiers as food and water, uniforms, and guns.

Her goal was to collect more books than existed in any single library in the world! Her motto was, "Let's do it!"

"Let's do it!" was the unofficial slogan for the big book drive. Using radio, newspapers, and posters plastered everywhere from schools to train stations, the largest book drive in American history was launched.

Safeway supermarkets placed book collection bins in all 2,400 of its stores across the nation. Hundreds of thousands of books were collected so fast—before the book drive was hardly underway—that the NDBC worried how they would manage such passionate book donations by everyone from schoolchildren to large publishing companies.

WE INTERRUPT THIS BOOK DRIVE...

On December 7, 1941, Japan made a surprise bombing attack on Pearl Harbor in Hawai'i. The United States was now at war!

The NDBC was renamed the VBC—Victory Book Campaign. Even President Roosevelt and his wife, First Lady Eleanor Roosevelt, donated books to the servicemen.

Pearl Harbor under attack, 1941

Now, the book drive felt even more urgent. Soldiers were headed out on trains and ships across the country and across the seas to fight. They would spend lonely, nervous hours clickety-clacking or splash-sloshing to their eventual posts. A book could make a soldier's probably first trip away from home more bearable.

Individuals and families carried books by hand and in boxes or grocery sacks to collection centers. Rich people piled books from their personal libraries in the back seats of their fancy cars or chauffeur-driven limousines to get them to the book bins. Celebrities, movie stars, famous singers, big bands—everyone helped announce the book drive and encourage the massive contribution of books, books, and more books.

The Gutenberg Address

Modeled after Abraham Lincoln's famous Gettysburg Address, a writer and actor, Christopher Morely, wrote, then read, his "The Gutenberg Address" on the steps of the New York Public Library.

**Johannes Gutenberg was the inventor of the first printing press in the mid-1400s*

Americans suddenly understood that World War II was a war of ideas, of freedom, and our democratic way of life. Mothers, fathers, teachers, workmen, writers, children—everyone realized what was at stake. Books were not weapons, but they were excellent tools with which to wage war against bad ideas, hate, and the miserable life that soldiers would endure for the next few years.

In two weeks, more than 400,000 books were collected, sorted, loaded onto Army trucks and sent to training camps and troops in transit to those camps. By the end of one month, more than a million books had been collected!

Although this was a lot of books, it was millions and millions too few to meet the need. What to do?

Poster encouraging rationing, 1944

Collecting Fever

During the war, many things were collected. Americans wanted to "do their part" to support the war effort. For example, they gathered spare aluminum for airplane parts, and families donated everything from coffee pots and dog dishes to watches and even artificial legs! Other types of items collected included rubber, paper, rags, and nylon stockings.

ration, rationing: to limit the amount of something someone is allowed to have, especially essential goods during wartime

What to Do?

The VBC asked publishers to donate books to help get to the 10 million book goal. Pretty soon, at least 4 million books had been collected. But there was a problem. Many people donated books that perhaps soldiers would not be too eager to read, especially while at war. For example, HOW TO KNIT. The VBC sold inappropriate books and used the money to buy other books more suited for soldiers. Children's books donated were sent to school or public libraries. Expensive, rare books, or first editions were sold and the funds used to keep piling up good books for America's fighting men.

Where Did All These Books End Up?

The millions of donated books were shipped as far and wide as the soldiers traveled—training camps, warships, posts, forts...to the Arctic Ocean and the Indian Ocean...to Africa, Australia, Iceland, Greenland, and hundreds of tiny islands in the Pacific Ocean. And later, to hospitals, where many soldiers were recovering from their wounds.

Everywhere the books went, they found soldiers who were tired, dirty, scared, and desperate for something to read. These soldiers said that they could read almost anywhere: in a hammock on a ship; in the jungle; in the gun port of an airplane; even in a foxhole filled with muddy water.

By day, or by night, with a flashlight or by moonlight, soldiers read. Sometimes they ran out of food rations, even toilet paper, but they just didn't want to run out of books. Every book that was read was re-read, or shared, until books were tattered and torn, and even then, they continued to be read until they just plain fell apart.

What did soldiers get from reading all these books? A moment of relaxation, a bit of escape from the battlefield, encouragement, hope, determination, faith, a laugh, a good line to share with a fellow soldier, new knowledge, and the reminder that not all in the world was blood and guts—that family and peace were still there, back home where they hoped to return one day.

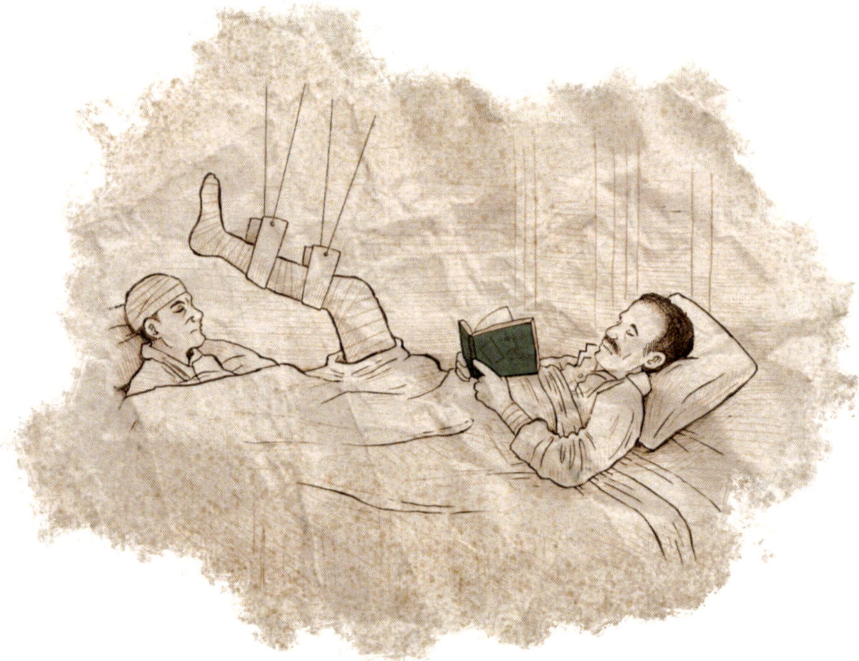

Soldiers who were wounded and found themselves spending days, weeks, or months in hospitals especially found the books helpful. A good book took their minds off their miseries. If the characters in the books were having a harder time than they were, it spoke to them in a special way and helped them feel not so alone. One soldier said he could easily prop a book on the elevated cast on his broken leg to read. And some soldiers read aloud to those who could not see to read for the bandages over their eyes. In many ways, a book was more important than a Band-Aid.

The Work Goes On

As the war went on, and books wore out, the work to collect more books continued. Soon more than 6 million books had been donated. The White House designated Friday, April 17, 1942 Victory Book Day. President Roosevelt was asked what types of books should be donated. He answered, "Anything except algebra!"

Books were considered symbols of democracy, free speech, and were a big part of the way that average Americans—even if they did not have a lot themselves—could help the boys and men so far away fighting for their country.

Girl Scouts and Boy Scouts collected books. One Boy Scout troop collected 10,000 books in one day! People would leave books on their doorsteps for the milkman to collect. One man in New York City pushed a rickshaw door-to-door until it was filled with books.

Soon, NINE million books had been donated for soldiers!

Next, the VBC begged colleges and universities everywhere to donate books. Remembering the many books that had been burned in Berlin, Germany, now nine years ago, these schools all rallied and rose to the occasion.

Soon, one million books more were collected. The goal of TEN MILLION BOOKS had finally been met!

Job Security

Think of all the jobs required to print these millions and millions of books. Which job would you have liked to do?

RESEARCHER WRITER EDITOR
TYPESETTER PROOFREADER
BOOK DESIGNER ARTIST
PRINTER BINDER PUBLISHER
PACKER SHIPPER

“More Books, *Please!*”

The numbers of soldiers continued to grow as the war waged on. Therefore, the number of books needed increased as well. But a couple of things made a big difference. One was that the soldiers, loaded down with equipment and traveling long distances in difficult circumstances, could no longer find room to add a hardcover book.

Another problem was that so many books had been donated, it was difficult to find more books to donate anymore, or at least not in large enough quantities.

Nonetheless, ever more soldiers begged for books. African American troops begged for books. Books were also sent to Japanese internment camps. The need for books was greater than ever.

Publishers generously donated all the books they could. Pocket Books were especially popular because they were smaller and lighter in weight.

Now that Americans had done all they could to collect books, many thought that it was time for the government to fund the printing of books for troops. In fact, new books picked just for the servicemen and printed in even more compact and lighter-weight editions—by the thousands—was what was needed.

A Big Challenge

What was needed was a big, new idea. With war rationings, book publishers had a hard time getting paper for their own publications. But they were determined to help the soldiers and so everyone put on their thinking caps and began to invent new ideas about what a book could be.

Everyone truly believed that books could help win the war. That books were essential. And that books were even weapons in the war of ideas. Publishers banded together to ponder the problem and see what they could come up with to solve it.

Soldiers were eager for different kinds of books. They wanted to know more about what this war was actually over, what they were fighting for. They were eager to learn more about the countries they found themselves fighting in. They wanted to better understand the people and their cultures. And, as always, they wanted hope, relief, encouragement, and a moment of pleasure and escape in their reading. Books mattered.

"The Armed Services Edition" of books was created. Books specifically for soldiers—wherever they were, whatever they wanted to know or learn about.

However, the challenge was not to find good books to print, but how to get them printed in a small and lightweight form.

A Bigger Challenge

Now that the government was involved, it provided 900 tons of paper every three months for the publication of Armed Services Edition books. Everything was designed for the soldier.

Books were made in smaller sizes that would fit in a back pocket, a jacket pocket, or a pack. Paper was thinner, so that the "paperback" books (something new in the publishing industry) would bend but not break. Paper was lighter in weight, so that a soldier did not feel the need to leave a precious book behind.

Books went from a big, thick, heavy hardcover to a book as small as a slim wallet! It was much like when we once had large telephones on a side table or a wall, until we got small, skinny, handheld cell phones. It made a big difference.

A printing press

Many creative ideas were used. Magazine presses let publishers print books "two up" and then cut them in half like a sandwich. Shorter lines of text were used so soldiers could read the book more easily. If books were not the same word count, blank pages were filled with puzzles, author biographies, and other interesting material, much to the delight of the soldier reader.

Pasting up a book

Books were bound with staples instead of glue. In the jungle or other damp locations, insects ate the glue, which destroyed the books.

Everyone worked hard to make the books perfect for soldiers. The books cost only 7-cents a copy to make, even less when larger quantities were printed.

Massive Math!

It took a lot of wrangling to figure out how to get books for the soldiers done.

It was a real publishing marathon! Here are some statistics.

50,000 titles of 50 different books were ordered by the Army and Navy.

Next, 1,200 more titles were ordered. 50,000 of each of these were printed.

For the Armed Services Series, publishers and printers devised this method:

Series A: 30 book titles were printed the first month.

Series J-T: 32 books in each series were printed each month.

Series Q-Z: 40 book titles were printed each month.

Since soldiers were still starved for books...

Beginning with the Q Series, each book had a print run of 125,000 copies..

For the W-Z Series, each book had 155,000 copies printed!

What the Soldiers Said...

Over the years, soldiers everywhere could not resist thanking anyone and everyone who had anything to do with them getting books during the war. They told stories of reading them around a campfire or watching them fall from parachutes down to them in the jungle or on the beach. They swore that they preferred the books to ice cream, cigarette lighters, and even sports equipment!

Soldiers said they were so excited when books showed up that they pushed and shoved one another just to get a title—it didn't matter what it was. They were happy to read any book and then swap with a buddy for another. In a tent, foxhole, hospital bed, cockpit, chow line, even on the front like with bullets flying...they read when and where they could.

One soldier said:

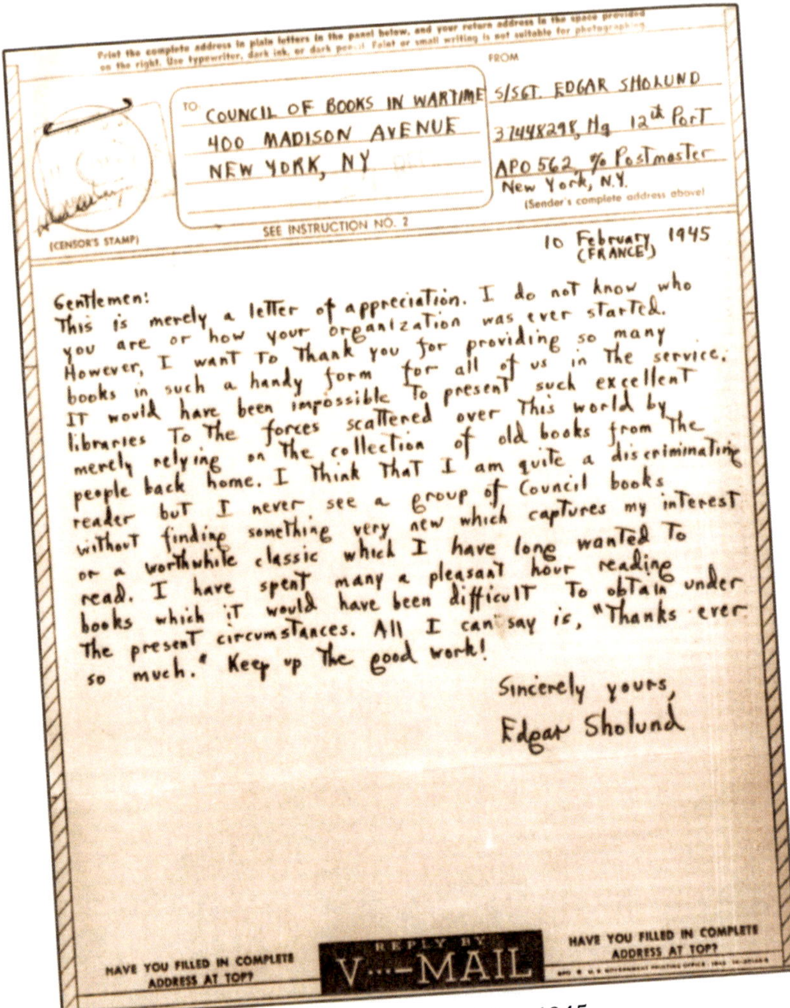

Print the complete address in plain letters in the panel below, and your return address in the space provided on the right. Use typewriter, dark ink, or dark pencil. Faint or small writing is not suitable for photographing.

(CENSOR'S STAMP)

TO COUNCIL OF BOOKS IN WARTIME
400 MADISON AVENUE
NEW YORK, NY

SEE INSTRUCTION NO. 2

FROM S/SGT. EDGAR SHOLUND
37448298, Hq 12th Port
APO 562, % Postmaster
New York, N.Y.
(Sender's complete address above)

10 February 1945
(FRANCE)

Gentlemen:
This is merely a letter of appreciation. I do not know who you are or how your organization was ever started. However, I want to thank you for providing so many books in such a handy form for all of us in the service. It would have been impossible to present such excellent libraries to the forces scattered over this world by merely relying on the collection of old books from the people back home. I think that I am quite a discriminating reader but I never see a group of Council books without finding something very new which captures my interest or a worthwhile classic which I have long wanted to read. I have spent many a pleasant hour reading books which it would have been difficult to obtain under the present circumstances. All I can say is, "Thanks ever so much." Keep up the good work!

Sincerely yours,
Edgar Sholund

HAVE YOU FILLED IN COMPLETE ADDRESS AT TOP?

REPLY BY V---MAIL

HAVE YOU FILLED IN COMPLETE ADDRESS AT TOP?

A real letter from a soldier, 1945

The Rest of the Story

Later, as the war grew worse, the battles more intense, and the death toll larger, you might think that books would be the last thing weary soldiers would be interested in. However, just the opposite was true.

As soldiers prepared to head into some of the deadliest battles of the war, they still craved something to read and managed to cram a book in with their gear.

As soldiers mustered for the enormous D-Day invasion—many loaded down with as much as 300 pounds of gear—the men coveted books. Therefore, books were brought into the marshaling areas, seemingly as important as bullets to morale. They considered these lightweight "weapons" essential.

Even famous World War II General Dwight Eisenhower read western novels to relax before battles.

Perhaps one of the most poignant sights of the war was wounded or stranded soldiers propped against the beach cliffs reading as they awaited rescue.

As one soldier said, "These little books take you away." If you could not escape the horror of war, a story could transport your mind to a better place for a little while. Books were called "rare pleasures" that could sweep away homesickness and sadness.

By the end of the war, more books had been distributed to soldiers than Adolph Hitler had burned.

Book Genres

The most popular book genres with the soldiers were the following. Which would be your favorites?

FICTION HUMOR MYSTERY
HISTORICAL NOVELS
ADVENTURE STORIES BIOGRAPHIES
CARTOONS CLASSICS FANTASY
HISTORY MUSIC NATURE
POETRY SCIENCE SEA STORIES
SELF HELP INSPIRATIONAL
SHORT STORIES TRAVEL

genre (jahn-ruh): a category of similar books

The End... and the Beginning

As the war wound down and soldiers began to return home, their reading interests changed. All they had known for years was soldiering. What would they go home and do now? What work were they skilled for or could they train for? Marriage, children—the young men wanted to raise a family and have a job and career to support their family. But the world had changed. What jobs were available?

As usual, books came to the rescue. New books published for them included such titles as *You and Your Future Job* and *Twenty Careers of Tomorrow*.

The war had changed everything. Advances in science and medicine, for example, created new jobs and new opportunities to do good things. Some soldiers were eager to return to the farm, or perhaps the family business. Many others were determined to be on the cutting edge of new engineering or science. To be the traditional lawyer or teacher were some men's dreams, while others—now accustomed to the drama of war—sought more exciting jobs, possibly with the FBI?

While it was a new beginning for soldiers lucky enough to return home, it was the end of the massive book program. However, it was not the end of reading, for the soldiers—now civilians—had learned that they not only liked to read...they *loved* to read.

The books they continued to be starved for could now be found in bookstores in Omaha and libraries in Charleston. And, if they were lucky, in the tattered and torn, but much loved, Armed Services Edition books, some tucked away and brought all the way back home as treasured souvenirs of their incredible experiences in World War II.

A story has been told of a soldier being shot in the heart, but not killed. Why? Because the bullet hit a book in his chest pocket!

For the Love of Books

Some soldiers had carried favorite tattered books across battlefields and all the way back home. Books reminded them that life was better somewhere else, and that if they were lucky, they'd get back to that better place soon.

Whether the books were serious or "swell fun," they made their mark on the minds of the men. Boys who may have read little in school soon found reading a privilege and a joy. Some soldiers read so many books that their interests increased and vocabulary improved, making them avid readers for the rest of their lives.

To say some men "lived for books" seems like an exaggeration. But as the war raged on, soldiers grasped for anything to help them keep going. War is ugly; it has been said, "War is hell."

Especially on the forlorn islands in the remote Pacific Ocean, soldiers felt alone, afraid, even fearful this could be where their lives ended. It's hard to imagine a book helping them out of such misery, but the soldiers insisted that even a moment to smile, laugh, think about something else, or read about faith, hope, or the good side of human nature was an enormous relief.

Books, some said, were like "rain in the desert" or a "box of chocolates."

When the war was over, the men continued to read to learn more about what had happened, about history, other countries, and other cultures. Their minds had been broadened.

Many soldiers felt that they were smarter after the war due to the extensive reading they had done on so many varied subjects. They were more interested in freedom of speech, the banning of books, and other issues. The men felt much more able to read, assess, and make up their own minds about what books told them.

No one seemed to think about giving up reading. Books continued to be treasures, valued in peacetime as much as in war. The men were still...starved for books.

The Story Never Ends

There have been celebrations of the amazing events that brought books to soldiers.

Sometimes publishers and authors got to meet the soldiers who enjoyed their books.

There have been discussions on keeping the books going. Why not?! We still have soldiers on bases, overseas, and on maneuvers, even if not at war.

It is fun to imagine what kind of books they might want today!

The Library of Congress produced a lovely documentary based on WHEN BOOKS WENT TO WAR. Author Molly Guptill Manning spoke with knowledge, stories, and emotion about her research for the book.

The Library of Congress also has a magazine that featured a story on the Armed Services Editions. It's nice to see that such a little-known amazing feat is being shared more and more today.

Can you imagine having been a part of the millions-of-books book collection? Can you imagine being a soldier who received a book just when you needed it most? Can you imagine that soldiers who could not read, learned to read. And that soldiers who could read, but had never bothered to read books, learned they loved to read books.

Even more importantly, when soldiers returned from war, they were not only eager to continue reading, they were eager to use the GI Bill to go to college. Many became the first in their family to get a college degree. This changed America forever!

There's Always More to Learn...

BONUS FEATURE REEL

A Mini-History of World War II

A bit of background to set the scene...

Yes, there had been a World War I.

Most of the nations in Europe had not recovered from that war. Many countries had high inflation—everything cost TOO MUCH! They had massive war debt to repay. There was a lot of unemployment = no jobs.

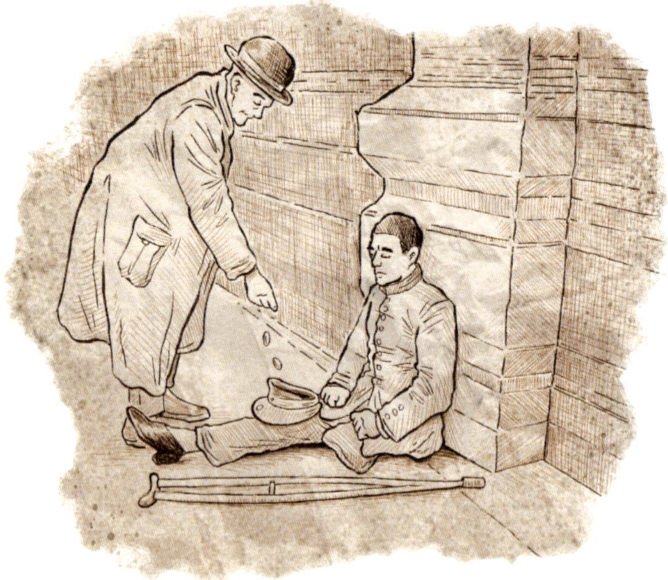

A wounded soldier after WWI and before WWII in Europe

Unfortunately, individual freedoms were threatened as dictators came into power in Germany, Italy, and Japan. These dictators were fascists. Fascism is when complete power is given to a dictator. The people have no say-so or freedom.

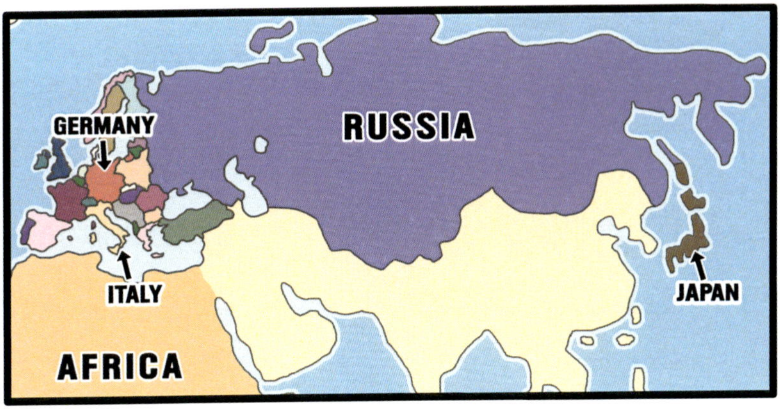

Map showing Germany, Italy, and Japan in 1939 before World War II began

These dictators set out to take over Europe, Asia, and Africa. They wanted to "conquer the world!" It might have seemed surprising that these three relatively small countries believed that they could take over much of the world and divide it among themselves. But they almost did it. In 1940 they signed a pact, an agreement that said that when they won the war:

- Adolph Hitler (dictator of Germany) would control most of Europe.
- Benito Mussolini (dictator of Italy) should rule over the Mediterranean and much of Africa.
- Hirohito (emperor of Japan) could claim East Asia and the Pacific for himself.

These were the AXIS POWERS. They were taking advantage of down-and-out nations while they were at a post-World War I low point. It was unfair. It wasn't very smart. But it wreaked havoc and started a chain reaction of death and destruction, the likes of which had never been seen before!

And now introducing the Bad Actors...

Adolph Hitler

In 1933 Hitler and his Nazi Party took control of Germany.

He insisted that Germans were better than anyone else and should rule Europe.

Benito Mussolini

An Italian dictator and journalist who founded and led the National Fascist Party.

Hirohito

Emperor of Japan during World War II.

Let the War Games Begin!

The Axis wasted no time.

- 1936 Mussolini invades Africa (the country of Italy is a lot smaller than the continent of Africa!)
- 1937 Japan invades China (Japan is tiny compared to CHINA)
- 1938 Germany takes over the country of Austria.
- 1938-9 Hitler's army moves in and occupies the country of Czechoslovakia.

And even though Hitler had signed a "treaty of non-aggression" with Poland, the German Army plunges into the country and takes control.

The awful kind of war that Germany took to Poland is called BLITZKRIEG, a sudden lightning fast and furious attack on the land and from the air where they can encircle the enemy on all sides and kill them where they are trapped.

HOWEVER, the British and French had seen enough to know that they were next. In 1940, they surprised Hitler by declaring war on Germany! How did Germany respond? They attacked and took over France!

Nazi soldiers marching "goose-step" style

Not everyone in the Axis countries agreed with their dictators; they just had no say-so in the matter.

Many Germans opposed Hitler and his ideas. In 1934, Hitler had more than 1,000 Germans killed in the Night of the Long Knives. And this would just be the beginning of his war against the people in his own country, especially the people of the Jewish faith.

And then comes... Kristallnacht

In 1938, Adolph Hitler ratcheted up his atrocities against Jews with Kristallnacht (German for Crystal Night.) On this night, more than 7,500 Jewish homes were destroyed and 400 synagogues burned. Almost 100 Jews were killed and 20,000 sent to concentration camps.

Jews were forced to wear a yellow star so that Nazis would recognize them, harass them, and round them up and kill them.

Hitler's army made the Jews abandon their homes and move into crowded areas called ghettos. They were forced to work as slaves. In 1942, Hitler began to implement his so-called "Final Solution" to eradicate the Jews. Taken by trains to concentration camps (death camps), Jewish men, women, and children were mass-murdered by being forced into giant ovens or poison gas chambers. More than six million Jews died between 1933 and 1945. This horrendous period of history is known as the Holocaust.

The term Kristallnacht came from the large amount of broken glass from the destruction of Jewish homes, businesses, and places of worship.

A destroyed synagogue in Berlin, Germany, 1938

Anne Frank in 1942

It is important to note that not all Germans supported the Nazi party or believed that what was done to the Jews was right. Indeed, there are many famous stories of those who tried to protect, save, or rescue Jews from the death camps. You may know the story of Anne Frank, who was hidden by a non-Jewish family in the attic of their home for years. Anne wrote a diary about her experiences as a girl in this tragic situation.

The Swastika

This symbol had been used throughout history in many places to represent life, sun, power, strength, even good luck. Hitler claimed the swastika as the insignia for his Nazi Party uniforms and flag. Soon this formerly benign symbol came to represent hate, violence, death, murder, and most especially, anti-Semitism—hatred of Jews.

The intimidating Nazi soldiers who marched in a "goose-stepping" stride spread fear, as did their straight-arm salute and cry of "Heil Hitler!"

Back to War...

Once France surrendered, England knew they would be next on Hitler's radar.

Close-up map of European countries before Germany's invasion began

Australia and New Zealand declared war on Germany, but they were far away. So was the United States, which proclaimed that it would remain "neutral" in the war at this time.

In the meantime, Germany invaded Norway and Denmark, Belgium, Luxembourg, and Holland.

And Then, the BLITZ!

Hitler was determined to conquer England and break the spirits of all the British people. This "Blitz" was the constant nightly bombardment of the city of London.

"Blackout Rules" meant everyone had to cover their windows at night with black material to make it difficult for German bombers to find their targets in the dark. Street lamps were also turned off, as were vehicle headlights and taillights.

How dark was it? So dark that people bumped into one another on the streets...traffic accidents were common since cars were almost invisible in the night...and people even fell off bridges or into ponds and drowned.

When aircraft were heard overhead or spotted in the sky, air raid sirens blared. To escape the coming attack, people ran to underground shelters beneath their streets. They hid from bombs in their cellars, beneath stairs, or even under tables or chairs.

Woman and child nailing cloth over the window to block light

Night after night after night—it was a miserable existence. Although bunkbeds, toilets, water, and snacks were provided in the bunker, it was still hot, crowded, and scary.

Each street had an Air Raid Warden. Their job was to send for fire engines and ambulances when needed, and to check for injured people and unexploded bombs.

The British were brave! During the Blitz they conducted bucket brigades of water to do things like save their beloved St. Paul's Cathedral. Parents often sent their children aboard trains to relatives and others in the countryside to keep them safe.

And, yet, the Blitz went on.

Hmm...and Where Were the Americans?

For a long time, the United States chose to be neutral and not take sides in this war. Then they adopted a policy of "isolationism," saying they did not want to get involved in conflicts between other countries. America was still recovering from World War I and The Great Depression. Nonetheless, the nation wanted to help in some way to stop Germany from conquering all of Europe. In 1941, the U.S. Congress passed the Lend-Lease Act so they could send weapons and supplies to Great Britain.

The U.S. military also set up bases in Greenland and Iceland to protect from German submarine attacks. Later, more bases were set up along the Atlantic coastline. After all, the U.S. could not be sure that war would not come to their shores.

America not only had to look at Europe to see what was happening, it also had to watch its back as Japan grew ever more aggressive toward China, Indochina, and Thailand.

On a calm morning when many were still asleep, the drone of Japanese airplanes hinted at the SUDDEN, SURPRISING, SHOCKING attack on the U.S. Naval Air Base at Pearl Harbor, Hawai'i.

In an instant, more than 2,400 people were killed and ships and planes destroyed in the disaster.

This changed everything.

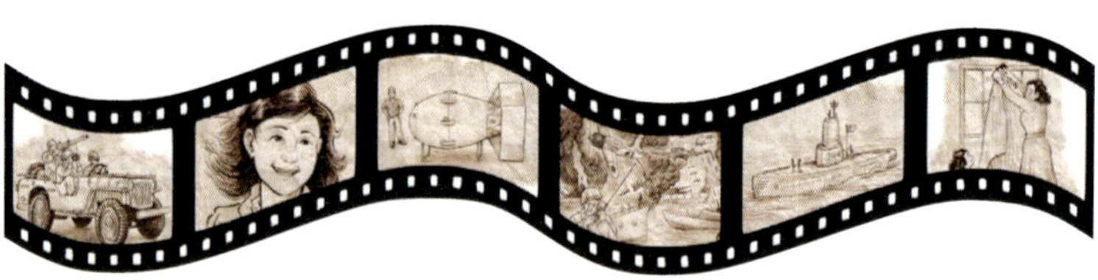

The next morning, U.S. President Franklin Roosevelt asked Congress to declare war, saying...

Overnight, the U.S. was no longer neutral—they were mad—and the nation was now at war!

MEET THE GOOD ACTORS...

It was like a football game...
AXIS vs. ALLIES!

The Allied Powers included England, France, the U.S., and Russia—all fought against Germany in World War II. Their leaders:

U.S.: President Franklin Delano Roosevelt

Then after Roosevelt's death, President Harry Truman

Great Britain: Winston Churchill

Russia (the Soviet Union): Joseph Stalin

While England was already suffering the Blitz and trying to fight back, and Russia was amassing troops, the United States was trying to play catch up, since it had not really expected to go to war. And it was not just the military, it was every citizen eager to do their part.

Women:

As soldiers enlisted and left in droves, women picked up the slack and served in every role the men had once held. On farms, in factories, running businesses. The most famous example was Rosie the Riveter, a muscle-flexing, bandana-wearing woman on a poster that said WE CAN DO IT! And do it they did, from building ships to airplanes, and much more. Women also enlisted as WAVES, WACs, and WASPs. Some helped as spies, code-breakers, cryptographers, and even went into battle and died.

Kids:

America's students soon discovered that there was much more to do than just hide under their school desks! As raw materials went to wartime needs, families had to "ration" or cut-back on typical household items. Maybe there would be peanut butter but no jelly, ham but no cheese. That's ok; feed the soldiers first. Even kids got ration books. Shoes, meat, gasoline, soap, and so much more were rationed, if you could get them at all. Kids helped collect much needed supplies: rubber tires; aluminum cans; and even ladies' nylon stockings. (Sorry, Mom!) Families planted Victory Gardens to grow fruits and vegetables to help those in need, and most everyone was in need.

Soldiers:

So many young men wanted to enlist in the Armed Services that lines were long. If the Marines were full-up, maybe the Army could take you. Navy—fine! Coast Guard or Merchant Marine, ok! Some boys lied about their age to try to enlist. Others were brokenhearted when they were deemed "4F" or physically unfit for service. Some boys were appalled when they were turned away if they could not read at a fourth-grade level. Most were recalled when the Army realized that they needed them bad enough to teach them to read!

African Americans enlisted and were a real asset to the war effort. One of the most famous units of Blacks was the Tuskegee Airmen. Once trained, these pilots proved to be smart, skillful, and courageous. They had the hazardous duty to fly alongside bombers and not one pilot was lost in over 200 missions where the Tuskegee Airmen escorted them. Even the fearless German fighter pilots feared what they called the "Black Birdmen." They were right to—the Tuskegee Airmen shot down more than 1,000 German aircraft!

Eight Tuskegee Airmen; above, their emblem

An Era of Invention and Ingenuity!

There was no time to waste! Every day, every minute was critical as war waged on. Just a few of the amazing and quickly-created tools of war included:

The Jeep:

Designed in just two days, this off-road vehicle was essential, even driving underwater! We still love our Jeeps today!

Tanks:

Early ones were more like big tin cans, but they improved rapidly and were battle essentials.

Submarines:

Deadly and silent...new and tough duty.

Aircraft carriers:

The ability to launch air strikes from anywhere in the world changed the way war was fought.

Radar:

Often called "the invention that won the war" this new technology offered a new ability to spot the enemy even at night and so be prepared to move out of the way or counterstrike.

A man records classified messages sent via radio.

Secret agents, spies, counterspies, ciphers, encrypted messages:

All these behind-the-scenes things gave a competitive edge to those who could use them best. The amazing Enigma decoding machine was truly an early form of computer.

The atomic bomb:

This discovery helped end the war and change the world forever.

The size of an atomic bomb compared to a soldier.

And things we now consider ordinary:

Penicillin; duct tape; the slinky toy; superglue; the jet engine; synthetic rubber; the microwave oven; and, as you know, the paperback pocketbook; and much more!

BACK TO THE WAR...

Germany was unrelenting:

- 1941: Invades Yugoslavia and Russia and continues to pound England with bombs.
- Germany soon controls most of Europe.

But the Allies are ready to fight back! However, it takes a long time and a lot of planning and complex logistics to prepare for their first battle.

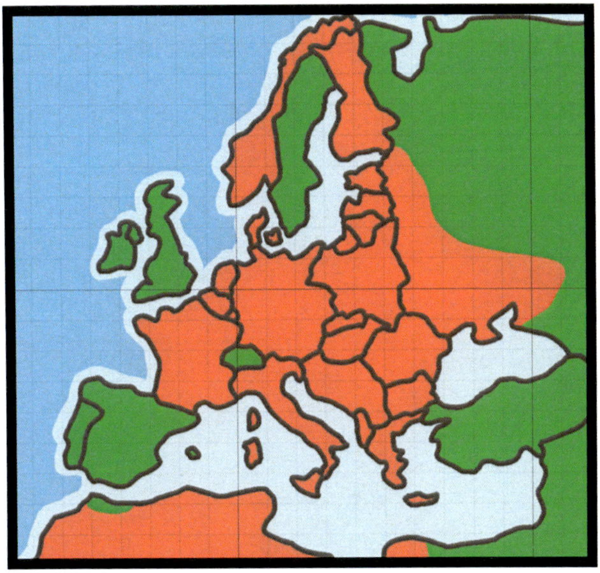

Map showing Nazi Germany at the height of its expansion in 1942: red shows land controlled or occupied by, allied to, or dependent on Germany

In the meantime...

It is difficult to explain how many heroic people—men and women, old and young—worked behind the scenes yet in plain sight during what was called The French Resistance. Most of these amazing stories were "classified" (not allowed to be shared) for 50 years.

Imagine...

You are a young mother with small children...you are a singing star...you are a princess...you are an ordinary woman with one leg...you are American, or British, or French...you are young, brave, but have never before volunteered to risk your life as a...spy.

We might think of spies as glamorous, but what these women resistance fighters were was courageous, fearless, and determined. Out there alone among Nazis on every corner, they had to play a role. But what they were actually doing was the impossible: making alliances with local French people (who also risked their lives) to organize air drops of soldiers and supplies by dark of night, trying not to get spotted by radar or the enemy.

For weeks and months, and often years on end, they lived a double-life, unable to share who they really were or what they were up to. They had no one to rely on but themselves and their "control" who would try to get them money and other essential supplies. That might mean medicine, weapons, or even red lipstick to fool the enemy into thinking they were one thing when what they really were was…deadly.

Not only did they evade Nazis and sneak large numbers of soldiers into the country to help fight the war, but they also risked their lives to guide fighter pilots (who had to bail out of their planes) across dangerous mountains in the dead of winter to safety in another country.

Many of these women were caught, tortured and killed by the Nazis. But many of them achieved amazing feats and lived, saved many lives, and helped change the course of the war.

Imagine returning home after such harrowing adventures and having to keep quiet about all you did for the rest of your life.

OPERATION D-DAY!

When the Allies finally struck they did it big! They had kept a major invasion top secret.

On June 6, 1944...60,000 Allied troops stormed the beaches of Normandy on the northern coast of France. It was the largest invasion by sea in history!

In spite of coming under heavy fire and losing many, many lives, the Allies took all five beaches and started a march inland to Paris. With the help of paratroopers falling from the sky, and many more soldiers, Paris was liberated, freed, and the Germans forced to leave France completely and for good!

In the meantime, the Russians were attacking the Germans on another front. Millions of their soldiers were killed, but the squeeze was on and Germany had to retreat.

Soon, Germany was forced to surrender. But that did not mean the war was over.

Famous photo titled "Into the Jaws of Death" - American troops depart from a Higgins boat and wade ashore to battle on June 6, 1944

Across the seas...

In the Pacific Ocean, Allied soldiers fought a grueling battle across an enormous swath of land and water. There were thousands of islands—hot, bug infested, filled with nasty water that let mosquitoes that carried the deadly malaria disease thrive. Thousands of soldiers died, but the rest fought on. Japan refused to surrender. Their kamikaze pilots were notorious for "suicide missions" where they willingly killed themselves to crash their fighter planes into U.S. warships.

Kamikaze, any of the Japanese pilots who in World War II made deliberate suicidal crashes into enemy targets, usually ships. The term also denotes the aircraft used in such attacks.

Iwo Jima

This famous WWII battle took place on a tiny island off the coast of Japan.

U.S. Marines invaded the island in 1945.

The Japanese had built an elaborate network of underground tunnels and traps across the hilly island. More than 6,000 Americans were killed trying to make it to the top of Mount Suribachi.

One of the most famous photographs of the war was of troops raising the American flag in victory.

February 23, 1945, United States Marines raise the flag on Iwo Jima

And yet, the war went on...

It was clear to the Allies that Japan would never surrender. To continue the war just meant many, many more lives would be lost. A tough decision had to be made.

Back in America, an atomic bomb had been created. This was the most powerful weapon ever known. Although no one really wanted to use the bomb, it seemed the only way to end the war.

On August 6, 1945, a B-29 bomber named the *Enola Gay* carried the world's first atomic bomb, called "Little Boy." The the 15-kiloton bomb (equal to the power of thirty million pounds of the explosive TNT) was dropped on Hiroshima, Japan. When it exploded, an enormous mushroom-shaped cloud ascended into the sky. More than 60,000 Japanese men, women, and children were killed, and even more than that wounded. Three days later, "Fat Man," the world's second atomic bomb, was dropped on Nagasaki, Japan. The death toll was very high. The world witnessed what an atomic bomb and deadly radiation could do.

Japan surrendered.

August 9th, 1945, atomic bombing of Nagasaki

The Rest of the Story...

Germany and Japan had surrendered.
On VJ (Victory in Japan) Day and VE (Victory in Europe) Day in 1945, the victors celebrated in the streets. The long war was finally over.

Adolph Hitler had committed suicide. A series of War Crimes Trials prosecuted Nazis who were found guilty of many atrocities, especially the death of six million Jews in the concentration camps.

The world tried to recover. The United Nations was created in hopes of helping nations to get along, work for peace, and avoid war.

EXTRA THE STARS AND STRIPES EXTRA

HITLER DEAD

Churchill Hints Peace Is at Hand

Left: newspaper from May 2nd, 1945

Below: People celebrate Japan's surrender on August 14, 1945

In the meantime...

Soldiers came home....families were reunited...everyone mourned the deaths of those who had not survived...and everyone continues to try to make sense of what happened, and how to avoid a WWIII.

Over the years many books were written about the war, many movies made.

World War II veterans were celebrated, interviewed, received awards, went to college, worked at jobs, raised families, and grew older. Of 16 million WWII soldiers, only about 100,000 are still living.

It's up to us to remember them, learn from them, and wonder how what they read during the war taught them, and what they can teach us today.

THE WORLD WAR II GAZETTE

Issue no. 2 September 1, 1939 - September 2, 1945 4 cents

LOGISTICS, NOT LUCK!

When publishers had to quickly decide how to create the perfect books for soldiers, they got creative.

Just because something has not been done before, does not mean that it can't be done. By working together with other publishers, printers, papermakers, and others, they came up with a great solution. Then, sort of like one big assembly machine, they had to figure out how to print, bind, pack and ship millions of Armed Services Edition books around the world as fast as they could!

Logistics: A plan and system of how to get something done the fastest and most efficient way, including each step, how to do it, how long it takes, and quality control. You can get a college degree in Logistics these days!

THE PROBLEM:

?

Small books
Thin books
Lightweight books
Same size books

THE SOLUTION:

1. Purchase Paper

2. Put Paper on a Diet!

3. Move Paper to the Printer

HOW TO PRINT AND BIND "SANDWICHES" OF BOOKS

HOW TO SHIP?

1. Box and Label
TO: FRANCE
TO: AFRICA
TO: NEW GUINEA
TO: NORMANDY BEACH
2. Load on Trucks
USAR
3. Trucks to Planes...
ARMY
4. Then...
BOOKS
BOOKS
BOOKS
It's a miracle!
Thank you!

A Victory Book Campaign poster from the American Library Association

Book Notes

Banned Books: Not only had the Nazis burned books by the millions, they banned many great books by authors from other countries, including America. And now, near the end of the war, here marched soldiers carrying the books that were banned across those "book starved" lands!

Give me an O; Give me an E: The U.S. Office of War Information had an idea. They would collaborate with publishers to create Overseas Editions (OEs) of many of the titles that they had printed for soldiers. The books had to be translated into different languages such as German, Chinese, French, Italian, and Japanese. More than three and a half million OE books were printed and shipped to other nations.

"I'll save my pages for you."—This is what one soldier said to another when books were scarce. One would read part of a book then tear those pages out and give them to a fellow soldier desperate for something to read. He could start the book while the other soldier finished the book, then passed those pages on.

Close to home: One soldier gave a book he'd just read this review: *"Hot stuff. That guy wrote about three islands I'd been on!"*

Soldiers said they learned to read fast when rain or snow was falling on the pages of their book. Some soldiers read as a group to save wear and tear on the few books they might have.

At one hospital, a doctor found a book on the operating floor. It had smudges of blood on the cover and on many pages. Seems almost nothing could keep a soldier from reading.

One military officer parked his car and later found it had been burglarized. The only thing taken was a carton of books.

Some exhausted and war-weary soldiers swore that books "*saved their sanity*."

Many soldiers wrote to authors, and many authors answered back. Some answered every letter they received. Others also sent autographed photos. One soldier even proposed marriage to an author!

One soldier said a book was like a letter from home, or even taking a temporary leave of absence from the monotony or horror of war.

Examples of Banned Books

Just a few of the authors banned by Germany during World War II included:

Ernest Hemingway
Helen Keller
Albert Einstein
Sigmund Freud
Jack London
Winston Churchill
and almost 10,000 others!

Examples of ASE books:

Oliver Twist by Charles Dickens
Typee by Herman Melville
George Washington Carver by Rackham Holt
Lord Jim by Joseph Conrad
Storm Over the Land by Carl Sandburg
The Fireside Book of Dog Stories by Jack Goodman
Chicken Every Sunday by Rosemary Taylor
My Friend Flicka by Mary O'Hara
The Yearling by Marjorie Kinnan Rawlings
The Adventures of Tom Sawyer by Mark Twain
...and hundreds and hundreds of others!

Questions to Consider

• You can't actually eat a book, so explain how a soldier could be "starved" for books. Have you ever felt "starved for books"? When and how?

• What does a book mean to you?
If you could NEVER get your hands on a book, how would you feel?

• Adolph Hitler was the head of the Nazi Party in Germany during World War II. He thought he could build a perfect race of people. One way he hoped to do that was by having people killed that he did not think were perfect. How does that make you feel about this man?

• Adolph Hitler burned a million books. He thought that if he burned those books, the ideas that HE did not agree with would burn with them. Do you think he was right or wrong about that?

• By watching today's current event news, we can see that a lot of people do not get along with each other. Many nations seem to prefer war to peace. How do you feel about that? Are there times when it's better to "get along" than to argue or fight? What roles do compromise and cooperation play in resolving conflicts, if any?

• Why do countries go to war with each other?
Is there ever a good reason to go to war?
Bad reasons to go to war?
What are alternatives to war?

• We imagine soldiers as being brave, fighting, and winning. The author describes soldiers as being sad, scared, bored, lonesome, nervous—can you imagine how and why they might feel that way? Does that make being a soldier sound less exciting?

• Do you ever take reading and books for granted? Why or why not? What if you were a kid in a school with no books, do you think you would appreciate having books more?

• The author says that some soldiers read as little as possible when they were in school before the war, but during the war, they often read. After the war, many continued to be avid readers. How do you explain this change in their attitude about reading? If you were a kid in a school with no books, do you think you might have changed as a soldier-reader?

• In this book, librarians are referred to as "super heroes" for collecting more than ten million books for soldiers. Do you think that makes them super heroes? How much time and energy and effort do you think librarians spent over and above their regular jobs and care for their families to collect all these books?

• Librarians were the first to realize that they could not have a successful book drive alone. Who collaborated with them to pull off the collection of ten million books? How important is collaboration in achieving a big goal?

• Even kids collected books for soldiers. Can one person, even a child, make a difference? If so, what might you do to help achieve a worthy goal?

• America did not go to war with Germany and Japan for a long time. However, they did begin to "prepare" for war, just in case. How wise was this preparation? In your answer, consider the difference between anticipating something, planning for it, and actually preparing for it.

• If you had been a man between the ages of 21-35, would you have:

a. Voluntarily enlisted in the armed services
b. Waited to be drafted

What might have influenced your decision?

• "Let's do it!" was the motto of the woman in charge of the great book drive. What is the difference between good intentions and actually doing something? How do you think Althea Warren led others to action by her influence and determination? What does the word *initiative* mean to you?

• In your lifetime there will be a number of significant events that change your life. For Americans, December 7, 1941, when the Japanese bombed Pearl Harbor in Hawai'i, was one of these moments. Some people describe September 11, 2001, when the World Trade Centers was bombed as one of those "change your life" days. Some people say they "grew up overnight" when such a significant event happened. How might you have felt if you had experienced those two days? In what way might such a dramatic event change your life, attitude, actions?

• Write a page in a diary of a young, never been away from home, soldier headed to war:

a. On a train across the country
b. On a ship sailing overseas

• World War II was said to be a "war of ideas."
Today, on the news, we see people argue over ideas all the time. Do you listen? How do you assess such arguments and draw your own conclusions? Are you ever surprised at your conclusions? Are your more of a follower, or do you try to discern what seems "right" to you, even if you are in the minority?

• There were a LOT of strategies needed to figure out not only how to collect millions of books, but how to sort, package, and ship them to the many places they needed to go. If this had been YOUR project, what strategies might you have employed to get the job done?

• During World War II, everyone said they wanted to "do their part." Which might you have chosen to do?:

a. Collect books and take them to donation centers
b. As a publisher, donate free books to the cause
c. At home, look around your house for extra paper, rags, rubber, aluminum, or other items that were needed for the war effort

In your opinion, can everyone do something? How do small efforts add up to big solutions?

• Surely all those soldiers, who came from different backgrounds and cultures and geographic locations, had to "agree to disagree"? What does that term mean? How important is it to listen to both sides (or many sides) of an argument and still be respectful even when you disagree?

• Why would a book be considered a "symbol of democracy"?
What is a symbol?
What is a slogan?
How can symbols and slogans be used for good or bad?

• When the challenge came to make books for soldiers smaller in size and lighter in weight, there had to be a lot of collaboration between the Army, printers, publishers and others. They had to keep an open mind about what a "book" could be. If you had been a part of this important project, which skills do you think would have come in handy:

critical thinking
the ability to analyze a problem
creativity
the ability to adapt
open dialogue with others
good decision making
the ability to solve problems

• Soldiers described books as "rain in the desert" or "a box of chocolates." How would you describe a welcome supply of books showing up just when you needed them most?

• How ironic do you think it was that soldiers actually carried "banned books" right into the countries that had formerly destroyed such books?

---

irony: when something is the opposite of what you expect it to be

---

• After the war was over, it was often quite difficult for soldiers to return home to "normal" life. They had to adapt to non-war conditions. While they had their "marching orders" in battle, now they had to make their own plans for their lives. They had to return home to families and compromise on decisions about the future. How important is the ability to adapt and change? How might you have felt as a returning soldier?

Glossary

Adolph Hitler: German dictator and head of the Nazi Party during World War II.

Allies: Nations who fought together against Germany in World War II (Great Britain, the United States, the Soviet Union, and others.)

American Legion: An association of U.S. war veterans.

Axis: Nations that fought against the Allied countries (Germany, Italy, Japan) in World War II.

censorship: Deciding, for example, what someone should or should not read.

D-Day: June 6, 1942, the day American forces stormed Normandy Beach in France during World War II.

democracy: A system of government where each citizen has a vote to choose their leader.

dictator: A government leader who runs a country and the people do not get to have an opinion.

free speech: The right of a person to say what they think.

internment camps: A type of prison where Japanese families were taken during World War II for fear they would spy for or otherwise support Japan instead of the U.S.

morale: The general spirt of a person or a group under certain situations.

overseas: A term that means abroad, over the ocean to foreign lands.

Nazis: Members of the Nazi Party, led by Adolph Hitler.

psychological warfare: The use of information or other tactics to confuse, discourage, or otherwise misinform people.

About the Author...

Carole Marsh Longmeyer is the CEO of Gallopade International, founded by her in 1979 in Rocky Mount, North Carolina. Today, she and her family create and produce social studies curricula for numerous states, as well as educational fiction, non-fiction, activity books, and more, including digital textbooks and audio books. Her work can be found in bookstores, museums, and libraries across America. The author lives with her rescue dog, Coconut, in Beaufort, South Carolina.

You may contact the author at carole@gallopade.com, or the publisher at www.gallopade.com.

Acknowledgement

In admiration of WHEN BOOKS WENT TO WAR by Molly Guptill Manning. Her rediscovery of this fascinating WWII history and her enthusiasm for the subject made me want to share the story with children.

A Note from the Author:

My father fought with the U.S. Army in World War II. It was his first trip away from home, first on a train, then on a ship. He was worried because he never learned to swim. He served in the Pacific islands, was wounded, and received a Purple Heart.

My husband was in the 82nd Airborne and later served 42 years in the U.S. Army Reserve's Chemical Corps. His older brother, 19, was a Marine, killed on the island of Iwo Jima near the end of the war.

We had a lot of other soldiers in our family, including my Aunt Ernestine who was a WAC (Women's Army Corps.) A nephew, Matthew, a Marine, a brother-in-law, Ken, who was in the Navy. And many others.

I have written a lot about World War II and some specific soldiers, such as Charles Dryden, a Tuskegee Airman. When I wrote his biography, he called and said, "You have made me famous!" I said, "No, Colonel Dryden, YOU made you famous." He answered, "But not with my nine grandchildren, and now I am!"

I often wonder if any of them were ever "starved for books" or read any of the donated books. If so, I would love to know which ones.

Resources

Library of Congress
Armed Services Editions Collection at the Library of Congress
https://guides.loc.gov/armed-services-editions-collection

Event Video: Molly Guptill Manning on When Books Went to War: The Stories That Helped Us Win World War II
https://www.loc.gov/item/2021689893/

The Library of Congress Magazine September/October 2015 edition
BOOKS IN ACTION: THE ARMED SERVICES EDITIONS
When books went to war, many American soldiers and sailors discovered the joy of reading.
By John Y. Cole, Director of the Center for the Book in the Library of Congress
https://www.loc.gov/lcm/pdf/LCM_2015_0910.pdf

University of Virginia
University of Virginia Library Online Exhibits
Books Go to War/virtual walk-thru exhibit on the 40th anniversary of Armed Services Editions
https://explore.lib.virginia.edu/exhibits/show/booksgotowar/walk/aseloc1

World War II: When Men, Women and Children Saved the World!
Carole Marsh
Gallopade International

The New York Times
How the Humble Paperback Helped Win World War II
A new exhibition tells the story of the Armed Services Editions, pocket-size paperback weapons in the fight for democracy.
https://www.nytimes.com/2023/10/06/arts/paperback-world-war-ii-grolier-club-nyc.html?smid=em-share

The following...

I.D.E.A.S.™

Inspiring Downloadable Educational Activity Sheets

on STARVED FOR BOOKS

...are available at Gallopade.com.

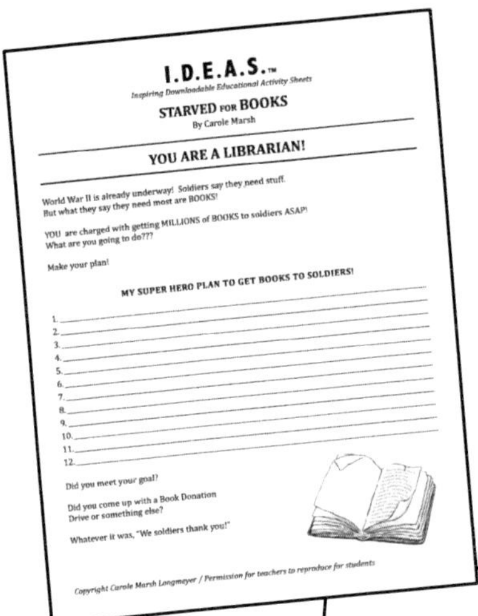
I.D.E.A.S.™
Inspiring Downloadable Educational Activity Sheets
STARVED FOR BOOKS
By Carole Marsh

YOU ARE A LIBRARIAN!

World War II is already underway! Soldiers say they need stuff.
But what they say they need most are BOOKS!

YOU are charged with getting MILLIONS of BOOKS to soldiers ASAP!
What are you going to do???

Make your plan!

MY SUPER HERO PLAN TO GET BOOKS TO SOLDIERS!

1. ____
2. ____
3. ____
4. ____
5. ____
6. ____
7. ____
8. ____
9. ____
10. ____
11. ____
12. ____

Did you meet your goal?

Did you come up with a Book Donation Drive or something else?

Whatever it was, "We soldiers thank you!"

Copyright Carole Marsh Longmeyer / Permission for teachers to reproduce for students

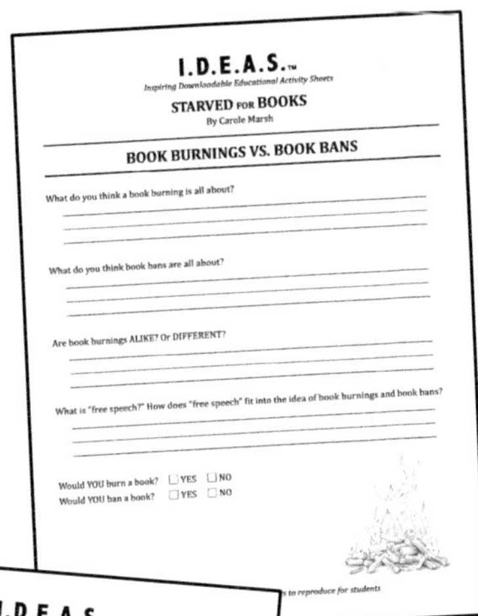
I.D.E.A.S.™
Inspiring Downloadable Educational Activity Sheets
STARVED FOR BOOKS
By Carole Marsh

BOOK BURNINGS VS. BOOK BANS

What do you think a book burning is all about?

What do you think book bans are all about?

Are book burnings ALIKE? Or DIFFERENT?

What is "free speech?" How does "free speech" fit into the idea of book burnings and book bans?

Would YOU burn a book? ☐ YES ☐ NO
Would YOU ban a book? ☐ YES ☐ NO

I.D.E.A.S.™
Inspiring Downloadable Educational Activity Sheets
STARVED FOR BOOKS
By Carole Marsh

WHAT WOULD YOU CHOOSE?

Think about it: The Armed Services Editions were on all kinds of subjects.
These subjects were chosen because soldiers asked, begged for them.

Imagine that you are a WWII soldier. Which book would you choose?
MATCH THE SOLDIER TO THE BOOK.

PARATROOPER
NAVY SEAL
FOOT SOLDIER
TANK DRIVER
WAC (Women's Army Corp)
GENERAL
WOUNDED SOLDIER
HOMESICK SOLDIER
MARINE
PILOT

MOM'S COOKBOOK
ALGEBRA FOR ALL
MYSTERY OF MAYHEM
A SOLDIER'S STORY
REPAIRING AUTOMOBILES
POETRY FOR THE AGES
ADVENTURES IN AUSTRALIA
BACK ON THE FARM
A LOVE STORY
CLASSIC GREEK MYTHS

Copyright Carole Marsh Longmeyer / Permission for teachers to reproduce for students

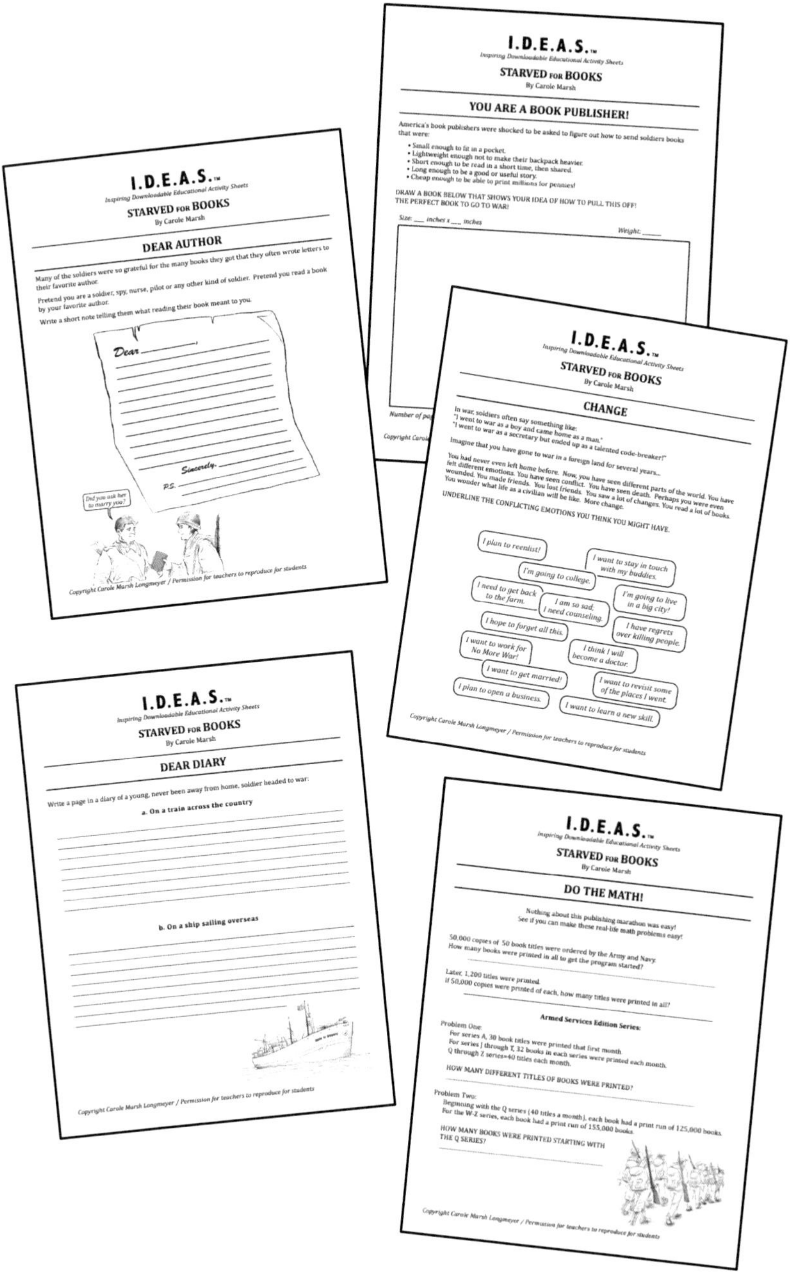

I.D.E.A.S.™
Inspiring Downloadable Educational Activity Sheets
STARVED FOR BOOKS
By Carole Marsh

DEAR AUTHOR

Many of the soldiers were so grateful for the many books they got that they often wrote letters to their favorite author.

Pretend you are a soldier, spy, nurse, pilot or any other kind of soldier. Pretend you read a book by your favorite author.

Write a short note telling them what reading their book meant to you.

Dear ______,

Sincerely,

P.S.

Did you ask her to marry you?

Copyright Carole Marsh Longmeyer / Permission for teachers to reproduce for students

I.D.E.A.S.™
Inspiring Downloadable Educational Activity Sheets
STARVED FOR BOOKS
By Carole Marsh

YOU ARE A BOOK PUBLISHER!

America's book publishers were shocked to be asked to figure out how to send soldiers books that were:

- Small enough to fit in a pocket.
- Lightweight enough not to make their backpack heavier.
- Short enough to be read in a short time, then shared.
- Long enough to be a good or useful story.
- Cheap enough to be able to print millions for pennies!

DRAW A BOOK BELOW THAT SHOWS YOUR IDEA OF HOW TO PULL THIS OFF! THE PERFECT BOOK TO GO TO WAR!

Size: ___ inches x ___ inches Weight: ______

Number of pa…

Copyright Carole…

I.D.E.A.S.™
Inspiring Downloadable Educational Activity Sheets
STARVED FOR BOOKS
By Carole Marsh

CHANGE

In war, soldiers often say something like:
"I went to war as a boy and came home as a man."
"I went to war as a secretary but ended up as a talented code-breaker!"

Imagine that you have gone to war in a foreign land for several years…

You had never even left home before. Now, you have seen different parts of the world. You have felt different emotions. You have seen conflict. You have seen death. Perhaps you were even wounded. You made friends. You lost friends. You saw a lot of changes. You read a lot of books. You wonder what life as a civilian will be like. More change.

UNDERLINE THE CONFLICTING EMOTIONS YOU THINK YOU MIGHT HAVE.

I plan to reenlist!
I want to stay in touch with my buddies.
I'm going to college.
I need to get back to the farm.
I am so sad; I need counseling.
I'm going to live in a big city!
I hope to forget all this.
I have regrets over killing people.
I want to work for No More War!
I think I will become a doctor.
I want to get married!
I want to revisit some of the places I went.
I plan to open a business.
I want to learn a new skill.

Copyright Carole Marsh Longmeyer / Permission for teachers to reproduce for students

I.D.E.A.S.™
Inspiring Downloadable Educational Activity Sheets
STARVED FOR BOOKS
By Carole Marsh

DEAR DIARY

Write a page in a diary of a young, never been away from home, soldier headed to war:

a. On a train across the country

b. On a ship sailing overseas

Copyright Carole Marsh Longmeyer / Permission for teachers to reproduce for students

I.D.E.A.S.™
Inspiring Downloadable Educational Activity Sheets
STARVED FOR BOOKS
By Carole Marsh

DO THE MATH!

Nothing about this publishing marathon was easy!
See if you can make these real-life math problems easy!

50,000 copies of 50 book titles were ordered by the Army and Navy. How many books were printed in all to get the program started?

Later, 1,200 titles were printed. If 50,000 copies were printed of each, how many titles were printed in all?

Armed Services Edition Series:

Problem One:
For series A, 30 book titles were printed that first month.
For series J through T, 32 books in each series were printed each month.
Q through Z series=40 titles each month.

HOW MANY DIFFERENT TITLES OF BOOKS WERE PRINTED?

Problem Two:
Beginning with the Q series (40 titles a month), each book had a print run of 125,000 books.
For the W-Z series, each book had a print run of 155,000 books.

HOW MANY BOOKS WERE PRINTED STARTING WITH THE Q SERIES?

Copyright Carole Marsh Longmeyer / Permission for teachers to reproduce for students

Also, a downloadable list of the **Questions to Consider** from this book is available at Gallopade.com.

Bibliography

Books

The Diary of a Young Girl
Anne Frank

The Attack on Pearl Harbor
Peter Benoit

World War II Resistance Fighters
Matt Doeden

World War II
Visual Encyclopedia

Snow Treasure
Marie McSwigan

Audiobooks

Twenty and Ten
French teacher and students take in Jewish children to save their lives

The Boy on the Wooden Box
Memoir of a "Schindler's List" child

The Book Thief
by Marcus Zusak

Number the Stars
by Lois Lowry

I Am David
by Anne Holm

Graphic Novels

MAUS
The Jewish Experience
Art Spiegelman

Gaijin: American Prisoner of War
The Japanese American Experience
Matt Faulkner

Night Witches at War
The Soviet Women Pilots of WWII

Navajo Code Talkers
Top Secret Messengers of WWII
Stuart A. Kallen

Documentaries

The War
By Ken Burns and Lynn Novick

Paper Clips
Students ponder the number of people killed in WWII

The True Story of the Bridge Over the River Kwai

Movies

The Monuments Men
How soldiers tracked down and saved priceless art stolen during WWII

Molly: An American Girl on the Homefront

Bedknobs and Broomsticks

Hope and Glory
A story of a British family during the Blitz

Life is Beautiful

Index

Image Credits

Poster, page 12 — "Books Are Weapons in the War of Ideas." Artist Steve Broder. 1942. U.S. Office of War Information. Image courtesy of the Franklin D. Roosevelt Presidential Library and Museum. Accessed October 8, 2023, https://fdr.artifacts.archives.gov/objects/15049/books-are-weapons-in-the-war-of-ideas.

Poster, page 13 — "We Can Do It!" Artist J. Howard Miller. 1942. National Museum of American History, Smithsonian Institution. Wikimedia Commons. Accessed September 24, 2023, https://en.wikipedia.org/wiki/File:We_Can_Do_It!.jpg#filelinks.

Photo, page 14 — "Penn Station Girl." 1942. Bettmann Archive. Copyright Getty Images.

Photo, page 22 — "Pearl Harbor, Hawai'i. A small boat rescues a seaman from the 31,800 ton USS West Virginia burning in the foreground. Smoke rolling out amidships shows where the most extensive damage occurred. Note the two men in the superstructure. The USS Tennessee is inboard." 1941. Library of Congress, Prints & Photographs Division, Farm Security Administration/Office of War Information Black-and-White Negatives. Retrieved from the Library of Congress. Accessed September 24, 2023, www.loc.gov/item/2017871935/.

Poster, page 25 — "Of Course I Can! I'm patriotic as can be - And ration points won't worry me!" Artist Dick Williams. 1944. War Food Administration. Special Collections, USDA National Agricultural Library. Accessed September 24, 2023, https://www.nal.usda.gov/exhibits/speccoll/items/show/245.

Photo, page 42 — "Sholund Letter." Edgar Sholund Correspondence. 1945. Council on Books in Wartime Records, Box 32, "Letters from Servicemen J–Z" folders, 20th Century Public Policy Records, Seeley G. Mudd Manuscript Library, Department of Rare Books and Special Collections, Princeton University Library.

Photo, page 58 — From front page of the U.S. Army newspaper Stars and Stripes announcing Hitler's death. Created by U.S. Army. May 2nd 1945. Accessed October 19, 2023, https://upload.wikimedia.org/wikipedia/commons/5/56/Stars_%26_Stripes_%26_Hitler_Dead2.jpg

Photo, page 58 — Portrait of Benito Mussolini. Accessed October 19, 2023, https://upload.wikimedia.org/wikipedia/commons/6/67/Mussolini_biografia.jpg.

Photo, page 58 — Hirohito in dress uniform. 1935. Library of Congress. Accessed October 19, 2023, https://www.loc.gov/pictures/item/2002721830/.

Photo, page 61 — Interior view of the destroyed Fasanenstrasse Synagogue, Berlin, burned on Kristallnacht; November Pogroms. Center for Jewish History, NYC. Accessed October 19, 2023, https://www.flickr.com/people/36988361@N08.

Photo, page 68 — "Franklin D. Roosevelt." Photographed by Vincenzo Laviosa. Created about 1932. The J. Paul Getty Museum, Los Angeles. Accessed October 19, 2023, https://artsandculture.google.com/asset/iQHA8LCrsSxF4Q.

Photo, page 68 — Portrait of President Harry S Truman. Photographed by Frank Gatteri, United States Army. November 1945. Harry S. Truman Library & Museum. Accessed October 19, 2023, https://www.trumanlibrary.gov/photograph-records/63-782.

Photo, page 68 — "The Roaring Lion." Photographed by Yousuf Karsh. December 30th, 1941. Library and Archives Canada. Accessed October 19, 2023, https://www.flickr.com/photos/28853433@N02/19086236948/.

Photo, page 68 — Portrait of Joseph Stalin. Created about 1942. Accessed October 19, 2023, https://www.britannica.com/summary/Joseph-Stalin#/media/1/562617/3641.

Emblem, page 70 — Emblem of the 332d Air Expeditionary Wing. Created by the United States Air Force. Accessed October 19, 2023, https://commons.wikimedia.org/wiki/File:332d_Expeditionary_Operations_Wing_-_Emblem.png

Photo, page 70 — Tuskegee Airmen. Created about May 1942 to August 1943. Accessed October 19, 2023, https://commons.wikimedia.org/wiki/File:Tuskegee_Airmen_-_Circa_May_1942_to_Aug_1943.jpg.

Photo, page 78 —"Into the Jaws of Death — U.S. Troops wading through water and Nazi gunfire." Photographer Robert F. Sargent. June 6th, 1944. Records of the U.S. Coast Guard. National Archives and Records Administration, Franklin D. Roosevelt Library. Accessed October 19, 2023, https://www.flickr.com/photos/35740357@N03/14353928304/.

Photo, page 80 — "Raising the Flag on Iwo Jima." Photographed by Joe Rosenthal. February 23rd, 1945. Accessed October 19, 2023, https://apnews.com/general-news-f00e1181d57a414a848ac96b772839fd.

Photo, page 81 — "Atomic Cloud Rises Over Nagasaki, Japan." Photographed by Charles Levy. August 9, 1945. U.S. National Archives and Records Administration, National Archives at College Park, Still Picture Records Section, Special Media Archives Services Division. Accessed October 19, 2023, https://upload.wikimedia.org/wikipedia/commons/e/e0/Nagasakibomb.jpg.

Photo, page 82 — Front page of the U.S. Army newspaper Stars and Stripes announcing Hitler's death. Created by U.S. Army. May 2nd 1945. Accessed October 19, 2023, https://upload.wikimedia.org/wikipedia/commons/5/56/Stars_%26_Stripes_%26_Hitler_Dead2.jpg

Photo, page 82 — Photo of residents of Oak Ridge, TN, celebrating the surrender of Japan. Photographed by Ed Westcott. August 14, 1945. U.S. Army. American Museum of Science and Energy. Accessed October 19, 2023, https://upload.wikimedia.org/wikipedia/commons/0/04/War_Ends.jpg.

Poster, page 88 — "We Want Books." Artist C.B. Falls. Victory Book Campaign / American Library Association / American Red Cross / United Service Organizations for National Defense Inc. Accessed October 24, 2023, https://digicom.bpl.lib.me.us/wwII_posters_hmfront/127/.

Poster, page 108 — "I want you for U.S. Army : nearest recruiting station / James Montgomery Flagg." Artist James Montgomery Flagg. 1917. Library of Congress Prints and Photographs Division Washington, D.C. Accessed October 25, 2023, www.loc.gov/item/96507165/.

JAMES MONTGOMERY FLAGG
I WANT YOU
TO READ A BOOK!